The Moon Telegrams

Volume Two

July 2021 - December 2021

Annaliese Morgan

First published in the UK by Black Daisy Press
49 Greek Street London W1D 4EG

www.blackdaisypress.com

© Annaliese Morgan 2021
The right of Annaliese Morgan to be identified as the author of this work has been asserted by her in accordance with the Copyright, Designs and Patents Act 1988.

All Rights Reserved.

No part of this book may be printed, reproduced or utilised in any form or by any electronic, mechanical or other means, now known or hereafter invented, including photocopying and recording, or in any information storage retrieval system, without permission in writing from the publishers.

This is a work of non-fiction, and the author has made every effort to provide accurate information and credits. Any inaccuracies or missing information will be resolved in subsequent reprints upon notification. Neither the author nor publisher is responsible for results accrued from any advice given in this book as it may not be suitable for every situation.

A catalogue record for this book is available from the British Library

ISBN: 978-1 8384163-4-8

*Still dedicated to all those who
ever wondered about life.
Never stop wondering.*

Annaliese Morgan is an English author for young and new adults. Originally from Yorkshire but based in London, she lives with her two sons, a Basset hound called Pineapple and too many books. Her writing career began back in the late nineties and has produced both non-fiction and fiction work. Annaliese primarily writes in the genres of urban fantasy and contemporary, and she has been featured on BBC Radio, Stage 32, Woman Magazine, Woman's Own Magazine, Stylist and many others. Annaliese and her two boys (often referred to as 'The Ms' or 'the three musketeers') are also avid travellers and a creative family doing life their own way.

Find out more at www.annaliesemorgan.com

Other titles by Annaliese Morgan

<u>Previous Titles</u>

The Moon Telegrams Volume One

Breaking Chains – autobiographical inspiring vignettes

Desperate Housepets – Become a chic pet owner without being a bitch

How to get through NVQ 2 veterinary Nurses

How to get through NVQ 3 veterinary Nurses A-Z for veterinary nurses

Anaesthesia and analgesia chapter in BSAVA Manual for Veterinary Nurses

<u>Forthcoming Titles</u>

Stay Wild

Rocked by Love

Contents

July 10th, 2021   1

8Th August 2021   7

7th September 2021   15

20th October 2021   22

4th November 2021   29

4th December 2021   36

Contact the Author   45

Bibliography   46

Introduction

At the end of 2020 I decided to create The Moon telegrams; free digital vintage looking vignettes delivered to subscribers every month on the day of the new moon. Each telegram interprets and explains interesting themes and subjects about the supernatural world, mythical beings, the Cosmos and ancient secrets. They are non-fiction, informative and open the mind to other realities and possibilities, or it might just twist it a little, as you start to ask bigger *why* questions about life and probe further into what is true and what isn't within our human existence.

They became more popular than I first anticipated and little treasures one can keep. It bothered me these pieces of work would eventually become lost in the slush of email bins, so I turned the telegrams to make into mini volumes.

You will find explanations on supernatural entities, mermaids, vampires, symbology, energies of the Cosmos, dragons, psychic abilities, ancient secrets that have been disguised for hundreds of years and so much more.

The point of The Moon Telegrams is to expand and enrich your life. To introduce you to your own mystical journey, ignite an unlit match within you or deepen your knowledge on which already interests you. Each of these telegrams are books and subject matter in their own right, so please know there is far more behind each telegram you can investigate, and I invite you to do so. The information in these telegrams can often be incorporated into *your way of being and life* too, aiding you to live how you wish to.

The Moon Telegrams are timeless and ageless and will apply at whatever stage or year you are reading these. You may read them all in one sitting, dip in and out or refer to them whenever you want or need to.

I have studied for decades on all these topics and areas of the supernatural, the mystical and esoteric thought. I am qualified in diplomas in many of these subjects (including vampirology, symbology, ancient Egyptian magic and dragons) and I have trained with the country's best psychics and mediums. For years, and still today, I am repeatedly asked for advice or sought out to answer questions about life and the unseen realms... I guarantee you have asked yourself questions about not only the meaning of your life but what else is going on, is there really a supernatural world and something bigger than I?

My answer is a resounding yes.

I hope I move you into an enchanting life,

Annaliese.

The Moon Telegrams

Date: July 10th, 2021
England

Hello to one and all,

I wanted to send a telegram on this new moon about an ancient communication and divination system which began around 2000 years ago (approximately 50 BC). The Runes.

The word Rune originates from mystery or secret and the Runes themselves are a collection of twenty-four symbols that were originally carved or etched onto wood, stone or bone... one reason as to why the symbols are so sharp looking and angular. These days the symbols are often etched on to more practical materials, such as pieces of crystal like onyx (more on this later).

Communication using Runes is an ancient tradition of the Nordic and Germanic people, including the Vikings. Runes formed their first writing and communication system, not only between each other (the symbols would be carved onto trees to leave messages for example) but as a way of receiving messages, guidance, insights and empowerment from the higher supernatural realms. The January Moon Telegram, explaining supernatural (psychic) guidance and the different portals we have in order to receive this, blends with reading the Runes.

Much is known, if not commercialised, about tarot cards and readings, wiccan spells and oracle cards but not so much about the secret magical mysterious Runes. The Runes are used these days in a similar way to tarot readings and you may notice Rune symbols on certain TV shows and movies. Many tattoos inked on bodies are, indeed, symbols of the Runes.

WHO INVENTED THE RUNE SYMBOLS?

In Norse lore there was magician God known as Odin, a Germanic Woden who gave his name to Wednesday, but Odin was also Lord of the Runes and embodied inspiration, wisdom, secrets, prophecy and communication.

Odin impaled his heart with his own spear and hung from the world tree – Yggdrai. He did this for nine days and nine nights to receive all the information, meanings and guidance of the Runes.

The symbols and each of their complex meanings was said to have come up from The Well of Urd (the source of fate) which sits below the world tree. Via and through the Runes, we too are able to access The Well of Urd and all it is potent magical information.

By the 5th century the Elder (old) Futhark Rune system was complete. The Younger Futhark system containing only 16 symbols followed, as the Vikings and other Nordic tribes developed them into less symbols but with deeper more complex meanings. It is though, the original Elder Futhark system that is mostly used today. In comparison, playing cards and the tarot cards didn't transpire until the 14th century and are not classed as ancient.

Runes today are widely sold. Usually in a material pouch with each symbol etched on either wood pieces, stone or pieces of crystal such as rose quartz or onyx. Mass produced Runes tend to be made of clay, take care to choose a substance which resonates with you. They essentially look like a bag of pebbles or small stones with a symbol etched on them. If you are purchasing Runes, buy from reputable Rune experts and make sure the symbol is etched on and not painted. Painted symbols can rub off. The material they are etched onto is less important than the <u>casting</u> of the Runes.

THE SYMBOLS

Below are the twenty-four symbols of the Runes. The top picture shows the symbols carved onto wood pieces. The bottom picture shows them etched onto crystal, most likely a form of Jade in this case.

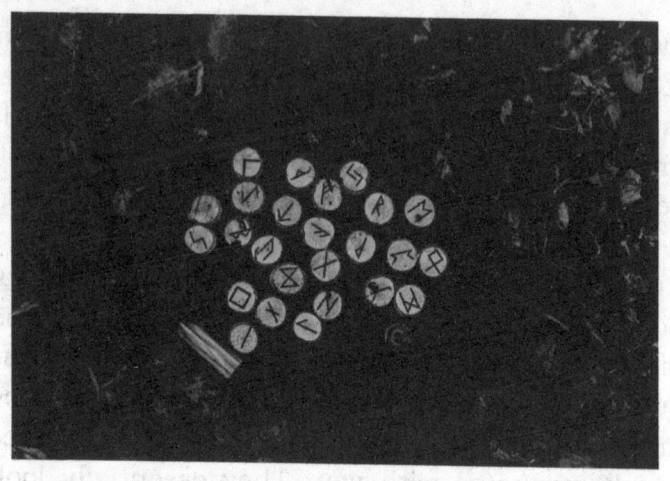

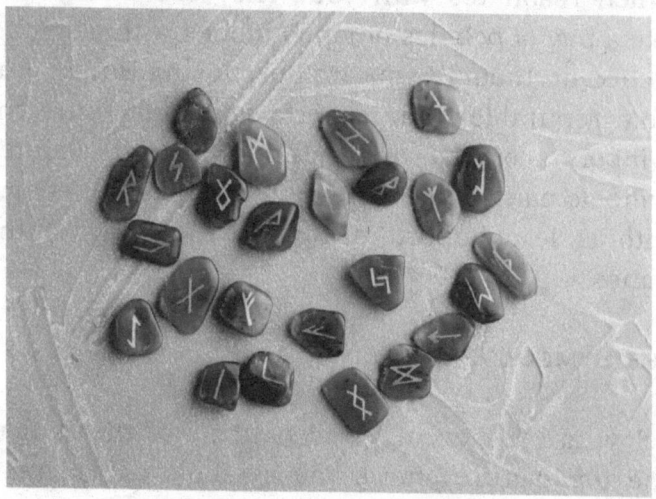

Each symbol represents almost a script of divinely sourced meanings, teachings and mystical guidance distilled into one individual symbol. There are Old English, Norwegian and Icelandic poems associated with each, as well the symbols' unique legend. Whilst Runes take time to learn due to their deep profound and complex meanings and insights, like most things, once you do, they are simple to understand and interpret.

You can learn to do Runecasting yourself or there are excellent and talented Rune readers and experts around (just less of them when compared to tarot readers and the like). Do your due diligence and research when seeking out a Rune reader.

RUNECASTING

Runecasting refers to both the spread and the casting of them.

Much like tarot cards there are numerous types of spreads and casting one can do with Runes. A common method is to throw or toss the Runes onto a white cloth or piece of material specifically used for the purpose of Rune casting and reading. The pattern in which they fall is observed. The symbols and placement of the staves (the individual Rune pieces) is then read.

There are more structured ways to perform Runecasting such as the simple Three Norn Spread... using three staves, that you were guided to pick from the bag, laid out as the past, present and future. All the way to more informative and deeper spreads like the Nine World Spread.

A Personal Favourite

One of my own favourite Runes is the symbol which looks like a bolt of lightening. It is called *Sowulo* and means the sun. It is a distinctly positive Rune and can be seen clearly on the second picture on the top left-hand side next to the Rune which looks like an 'R'.

A brief understanding of Sowulo

Sunlight gives power, growth and life to everything. It is a happy and positive symbol representing joy, growth, abundance, luck, good fortune, celebration and success. It is our higher self (and our source) radiating on to us. It also encases the cosmic energies and enlightenment and represents the hidden force expanding each of us daily. The Power in Norse mythology was often given to the sun.

This symbol cannot be read in reverse.

I hope this has given some interesting insight and intrigue into an arena you may or may not have been aware of. The power, answers and information we seek has being around us for thousands of years... ask Odin.

May the brightness of summer and Sowulo shine on you all,

The next telegram will arrive 8th August 2021.

The Moon Telegrams

Date: 8ᵀᴴ August 2021,
England

Hello to one and all,

This is an auspicious and most powerful day. It is the new moon AND the peak of the Lions Gate Portal... an astrologically happening which peaks every year on the 8th of the 8th with great effects and opportunities for humans. I firstly would advise, to get your thinking into positive order and to write down all your clear intentions and desires. Secondly, in this month's telegram, I bring you lucky charms to assist you on your journey.

Who doesn't love a lucky charm?

Many of us have something we consider lucky, whether it's a talisman sourced from a different culture or a pair of lucky socks. This August we delve into the origins of lucky charms and what these can bring to your life and why.

Lucky charms include the following: mascots, charms, amulets and talisman.

DESCRIPTIONS

<u>Mascot</u> comes from the French term *masco*, meaning witch. A mascot is a person or a thing that brings good luck.

<u>Charm</u> originated from the Latin word *carmen* which means song or incantation. A charm is a chanting of magical words or use of a magical spell leading to becoming enchanted.

<u>Amulet</u> comes from the Latin word *amuletum*. An amulet is a natural item or material, examples include: a tooth, stones, a bag of stones, botanicals, crystals/gemstones such as tigers' eye and horseshoes. Amulets are either carried or worn by a person. They protect and defend the person against the Evil Eye, negative energies, danger, illness and ward off anything with dark intentions.

<u>Talisman</u> originated from the Greek word t*elesma* meaning a blessed object. A talisman is a single item and can be a stone, a ring, a pendent or another object. Amulets can be used as talismans, but a true talisman must have an inscription on it composed of either words, letters, numbers, symbols or a pattern.

Talisman are assigned magical powers from the source, entity or deity relating to the inscription. The source can be supernatural, celestial, astrological, saintly or religious. They bring the wearer or keeper positive energies, magic abilities and good fortunes. They also offer protection like amulets.

You may often see amulets and talisman used in TV shows, films and books, the huge Netflix series Vampire Diaries for example. Many people create they own talisman either for personal use or for stories they may write... as I have done for my forthcoming fiction books.

Before we move on to examples of amulets and talismans, I want to briefly mention the Evil Eye; a term I'm sure you've heard at some point.

THE EVIL EYE

The Evil Eye is a malevolent force which transmits harm and negativity to a person simply by another (who has the Evil Eye) staring at the innocent person.

To avoid being effected by the Evil Eye or to survive it's attack, you can either disrupt the eye contact, avoid eye the contact, wear or keep hold of an amulet or talisman to protect you from it.

There are three types of Evil Eye:

- The innocent or unconscious Evil Eye – someone who is unaware and doesn't intentionally mean to cause harm or badness yet seems to cause negative effects or tragedy after their visit.
- The malicious Evil Eye – someone with the Evil Eye who causes harm and darkness on purpose.
- The unseen Evil Eye – a hidden dark invisible force and the most feared form.

Get yourselves some sort of amulet or talisman people!

AMULETS

The Cowrie Shell

Cowries are small sea snail shells and one of the most ancient of types of amulets, having been used as an amulet for over 10,000 years. Cowries were used by the ancients mainly as a form of money but also as jewellery and decorations. Today they feature in many a mermaid story and in a plethora of jewellery and decorations.

Symbolically the cowrie shells represent prosperity, wealth, fertility, protection and rank. Historically they hold much significance. In ancient times, Africa and China used cowrie shells as their form of currency. The Chinese also placed the shells inside tombs to afford the dead a wealthy afterlife.

Other civilisations saw the cowrie shell

representing an eye. In Egypt and New Zealand for example, cowries were placed in the eye sockets of a deceased person to give them sight in the afterlife. In other countries, headdresses would be covered in cowries creating a wall of staring eyes or they would be used to symbolise rank by the chief of tribes in places like the Fiji Islands.

India hung the shells around the necks of their cows or placed the cowries on the cow's forehead to protect them (cows are scared in India). Indian astrologers would also use them to aid their astrological interpretations and to predict the future.

Others, however, saw the cowrie shell as representing the female genitals. From this perspective the cowrie shells protect against infertility, undesirable/traumatic childbirth whilst promoting fertility and safety of both the woman and the child. They were used extensively in ancient Egypt over 5000 years ago and is another example of the ancient Egyptian magic I wrote about in the April's Moon Telegram. Cowries would often be worn around the pelvic and girdle area. In Japan it was custom a mother would hold a cowrie whilst giving birth.

Many pendants, dream catchers, jewellery and other oddities are embellished with cowrie shells. Now you know why.

The Blue Eye

The Blue Eye is not the Evil Eye but protection from it as it dispels its curse.

They have been around for thousands of years and originate from Turkey; tourists and travellers may be familiar with this one.

In Turkey it is known as *Nazur Boncuk,* or Evil Eye Stone. You can see them hung in cars, as ornaments in houses, within jewellery or as keyrings. There are numerous designs, especially these days, but they will always have one eye and be in the colour of blue. The Blue Eye provides protection from the Evil Eye, misfortunes, negativity and gives spiritual protection in general.

TALISMAN

These are a single item usually made of stone, metal or parchment, which enables the talisman to be inscribed or engraved. The importance of the inscription is because it's meaning, regardless of whether the inscription is words, symbols or numbers, will be understood by any unseen force, Spirit or power.

I wanted to bring your attention to a magical word used as an inscription on a talisman. It is also repeatedly used in stories, shows and games and in my opinion, it's true meaning has become somewhat diluted or misunderstood along the way. It's a great one to use and the word is...

Abracadabra.

Abracadabra originated from the Aramaic phrase *Aura Kehdabra* 'I will create as I speak'.

Remember the Ancient Egyptian Magic telegram from April again? The ancient Egyptians also considered their words (and spells) to be of the upmost importance because words create one's reality. As a further reminder, it is called 'spelling' for a reason, we learn to 'spell'...

Aramaic is a language created by the Arameans in an ancient region of Syria. It first appeared in the 11th Century BC and preceeded the Arabic and Hebrew languages. Aramaic is the oldest continuously written and spoken language of the Middle East but was eventually replaced with Greek.

What would you inscribe on your talisman?

There is plenty information online and books on this topic should you wish to discover more of these magical charms or send me an email I will always help!

In the month of August, particularly if you are travelling or visiting different locations, keep an eye out (pun intended) for any amulet or talisman you resonate with. Or start to notice where you see them. There are many different kinds, and you will likely now spot them more frequently either on people's jewellery, in their homes, cars or places of work.

Have an enchanting August!

The next telegram will arrive September 7th.

The Moon Telegrams

Date: 7th September 2021,
England

Hello to one and all,

Welcome to autumn or fall depending on where you are from. The season of pumpkins, woolly jumpers, long boots and a colour wheel of oranges, browns, and yellows. It is the season were the old is shed, as trees demonstrate, and the time of harvesting the years good.

Autumn is the time of year to shed the old and worn out and gather our harvests from the seeds we have planted over the last year. To do this though, direct answers and clarity are required. How can we gain such direct answers when we simple don't know what to do, are unsure, there are two choices or confusion dominates like a gothic storm?

I bring to you on this new moon a telegram about a topic which can help.

Divination using pendulums – a method to receive answers *right* <u>for you.</u>

DEFINITIONS

The definition of these words, as stated by The New Oxford Dictionary (1998), are as follows:

Divination – The practice of seeking knowledge of the future or the unknown by supernatural means.

Pendulums – A weight hung from a fixed point so that it can swing freely backwards and forwards.

There are numerous ways to receive answers through divination, and we have already looked at a few in previous telegrams but using pendulums for this is a simple and direct technique delivering an immediate answer. Pendulums are also relatively easy to master.

Answers we seek rarely come from outside ourselves; we already know the *right* answer even if we think we don't. Seeking the advice of another is seldom helpful because their advice or solution is what works for *them* in *their* universe, not yours. The exception here is when supernatural guidance is given to you via someone else, but this is usually heard by you off the cuff, or by overhearing someone and you are taken off guard a second when you feel the ping of truth. This is different from partaking in a detailed discussion with a person... where essentially you are looking for validation or permission from someone else to do the thing.

Proper answers which are true and real for you come from within, from your intuition, higher self, and guides. Using a pendulum is great way to access this as it helps get your mind out of the way enabling the channelled answer to emerge.

Pendulums (like the picture below) have a weight at one end, usually a crystal but can be a bead, a ring, a key, or any object that is not magnetic and has some weight to it. It is attached on the end of chain (or other material).

HOW DO THEY WORK

Pendulums work by communicating with your intuition and higher self and it channels that energy. When you ask *it* a question it will deliver a simple yes or no response by swinging or circulating in certain directions.

Pendulums can also be used for healing, discovering allergies, or finding missing objects. For the purposes of this telegram we are only looking at using them for receiving answers.

How to Choose a Pendulum and what do with your New Piece of Joy

The pendulum you choose (or make yourself) must be one you feel drawn too or connected too. If you resonate with a certain crystal choose this. There are multiple options, and they are easily bought online or in certain shops. Make it personal, sacred and yours.

Your new pendulum needs to be cleansed of any other energies, from other people who have handled it before you for example. This is done by placing it sunlight for a day, smudging it with sage or washing it in spring water.

Following this, charge it with your own energy so it can channel and translate your mystical blueprint. This is done by carrying it about your person and in your spaces for 24 hours. Hold it your hands for a good amount of time, place it in your pockets, under your pillow, on your desk, anywhere on or nearby you so it can absorb your energy.

Keep it in safe or special place. Do not let other people touch it or use it. If this happens, repeat the above steps as though you have just bought it. No one wants mixed answers because the pendulum has two different energies and charges!

How to Use It

Pendulums can only give simple yes or no answers. It can't answer in chapter and verse like humans. This is beneficial because it causes one to become focused, and to break a matter down into simpler smaller questions which then can be built upon.

1. Relax! Divination cannot work in a stressed, chaotic, or closed mind state. Meditate for 5 minutes before you start... practice deep breathing or something which slows you down. Keep an open mind and suspend your beliefs.

2. Hold the top of the chain in your <u>non dominate hand</u>, let the fingers of your other hand run down the chain and then lay that hand palm up underneath the now dangling pendulum.

3. Ask the pendulum 'give me an answer for yes'. It will begin to swing or circulate in a particular direction.

4. Then ask the pendulum to 'give me an answer for no'. It will begin to swing or circulate again but in a different direction to the yes response.

5. Next ask the pendulum 'do you want to work with me'. It will move in the yes or no directions you have just clarified. If yes continue, if no choose a different pendulum as it's the wrong choice for you.

6. Now ask the pendulum a question you know is true... 'do I live in the USA?' Check how it swings. Then ask a question you know is false... 'do I have blonde hair?' Check its response. This gives you evidence literally in your hand. You can repeat this until you are certain.

7. Then begin to ask your questions and receive your answers. Examples of questions could be, 'Should I move', 'is pasta good for me', 'should I sign X deal', 'Should I sign Y deal' and so on.

8. When finished, always thank your pendulum and place it back in its special place.

Pendulums are fun and a super interesting tool to use. You can tangible see the supernatural at work and you know without doubt it is not your hand or fingers making it move.

Swing gallantly through September telegramers!

The next telegram <u>will not</u> arrive on the new moon happening on 6th October, but on the full moon happening on 20th October, as it I feel it will be more fitting and celebratory for the topic of the October Telegram.

The Moon Telegrams

Date: 20th October 2021,
England

Hello to one and all,

Welcome to the full moon of October and a spooky telegram featuring what are considered, ancient creatures – Vampires.

1000's of stories about these intriguing creatures have being (and will continue to be) written and made into books, film, television shows and computer games. Vampires in our modern era, thanks to stories such as The Lost Boys, Twilight and The Vampire Diaries have given vampires a new romantic magnetic edginess. Often attractive rather than grotesque as they were originally portrayed. In our world today, vampires have an alluring fascination around them, even a sexiness to them. But where did vampires originate from, what are their traits and is there any truth to them?

Vampires are corpses who rise from their graves at night. They prowl around during the dark hours to haunt other humans, or to remain among them, and feed by drinking the blood of humans and in some cases animals and livestock. This is essential to sustain their new life as a vampire.

The first written evidence about vampires can be found in a poem which mentions the creature and was written back in the 1700's. It is widely thought vampires originated in Transylvania; however, this is not true. They originated from Eastern Europe, namely from the Slavic people and vampires are based on Eastern folklore. Many believe the vampire is jealous and bitter of those still alive and if sudden multiple deaths occurred within a family or village, a vampire would be suspected. One modern explanation of such sudden deaths is that it occurred because of a disease outbreak.

According to Slavic lore, a person who becomes a vampire after their death has an invisible shadow around their corpse for 40 days, which as they feed on blood grows in strength, and the shadow eventually turns to a jelly boneless structure until the body looks like it did before they died. Many tactics were used to prevent suspect corpses from rising from their graves and indeed modern archaeologists have discovered many old graves and coffins across Europe with these measures in place.

It is worth mentioning, male vampires could also engage in sex with female humans. Should a child be born from the coupling the said child then possesses special vampire hunting talents and can track and slay vampires. These children were seen as heroes.

Who becomes a Vampire?

The following reasons are said to be the causes why some people became vampires:

- Practising witchcraft or sorcery
- Physical disfigurement
- A strange birth, example a child born with teeth in their hair
- Those who have committed suicide
- A child of a vampire
- Having red hair
- Talking to yourself
- Neglected religious beliefs
- A dead body being leapt over by a black cat

Traits of Vampires

Vampires have certain traits, and these have grown as the decades and centuries have rolled on. Listed below are a few of the core ones:

- In folklore, vampires dress in what they died in, their eyebrows meet in the middle and their fingers are all the same length
- They need to drink blood
- They are immortal
- They have supernatural powers such as flying
- They are powerful, strong, and fast
- They can be killed by fire and a stake

through the heart
- They must be invited into a house or building to be able to enter it, after which they can come and go as they please
- They can't enter a church or any holy place
- They can't be seen in a mirror, which began in Bram Stoker's Dracula
- They sleep in the day as they dislike sunlight – this trait began in the Nosferatu film in 1922

RECOGNISING A VAMPIRE

Aside their traits, there are a few other obscure ways to recognise a vampire used by ancients and many since... just in case they don't rock up in grandeur like The Salvatore brothers (Vampire Diaries) or Edward Cullen (Twilight) and you'd like to be sure!

- If a suspect's grave is opened, even years after their death, their corpse will be unusually intact
- They are often unexpected deaths of family or animals
- They return at night and may eat food or knock things around
- Female vampires often return to be with their children
- Their activity continues even after a priest reads holy words and verses at their grave

- There is a hole the size of a serpent on their gravestone. The size needed for a vampire to exit
- A white horse will not walk over the grave of a vampire

How to Repel a Vampire or Inhibit a Vampire from Rising

Whilst each of the following has an explanation as to why and how, it's beyond the space available here to do so. If you are ever concerned about the proximity of a vampire, or prefer to inhibit them in the first place, reach for one of these solutions:

- Place a brick or stone in the corpse's mouth when burying them. Archaeologists have found numerous vampire graves where corpses have been buried in this way
- Bury them at a crossroads – it confuses vampires
- Decapitate the head of the corpse and place the head between its feet, or behind its buttocks in the coffin. Garlic can also be placed in the mouth of the head
- Garlic
- Hawthorn
- Holy water
- Religious symbols such as the Crucifix and The Star of David
- Fire

- Roses – wild roses placed on the top of the coffin stop the vampire leaving it without harming them
- Salt or seeds
- Sunlight
- Wine
- A wooden stake

As I bring this telegram to a close, which is tricky as it's a topic I could write a lot about, I want to leave you with something to ponder. I can't decide whether it's interesting or disturbing so I shall leave that decision to you.

REAL VAMPIRES TODAY

Vampire subculture overlapped with the goth subculture (goth subculture began in the 1980's in the UK). Those involved with vampirism (i.e. consider themselves to be an actual vampire) believe themselves to be superior and challenge anything restricting their freedom. They do not dress like vampires and keep their identities hidden They believe one is born a vampire and 'turning' (turning an ordinary person into a vampire) is frowned upon.

There are two sets of real vampires in society today:

The Sanguinarias – these exchange blood
Psychic vampires – these exchange psychic energy

The sanguinarias exchange blood following an official contract being set up and use implements such as surgical scalpels or razors. No teeth are allowed and 'donors' are used for the blood exchange.

Real vampires tend to live in the larger cities like London, New York (in particular, Manhattan) and New Orleans. Societies, including gatherings, special vampire clubs and courts exist everywhere. A special society for vampires has been around for some decades in the UK and a vampire research centre exists in New York. It is estimated that in 2015, the UK has 15, 000 real vampires.

On that note, I wish a happy full moon to you all. Please release all that which no longer serves you and watch out for vamps... unless you are one of course!

Have a blessed Halloween,

The next telegram will arrive November 4th.

The Moon Telegrams

>Date: 4th November 2021,
>England

Hello to one and all,

November is upon us, how quickly the months and time go. It doesn't seem two moon minutes ago the first telegram was sent out during one of a many Covid's lockdowns in January. I hope your year end is faring well as we begin to reflect on the year past.

I wanted to return to the telegram in January on psychic guidance and mediums as firstly I promised I would, and secondly to send further insight on how you can develop your skills for receiving supernatural guidance. Whether for yourself and personal use, or for reading other people.

Let's refresh ourselves on the different ways and portals we mortals receive this guidance, or if you are reading somebody else, how you translate their energy for information.

HOW DO WE RECEIVE OR DOWNLOAD PSYCHIC GUIDANCE AND INFORMATION?

There are four main ways. Usually, two of these are stronger and therefore we are 'better at' (these can swap about) but all four are always available to us.

Clairvoyance – 'Clear Seeing.' Often known as the third eye or mind's eye. A person with this skill will, in their head, see images, colours, and symbols. Anything visual. This is open to interpretation, which is why practice is important to correctly translate the meaning of the symbolic images you are given. It plays out like a screen on the inside of your forehead. Some with this skill see orbs and spirit forms in normal waking life.

Clairaudience – 'Clear Hearing.' A person with this skill can hear voices, whispers, singing or sounds in general. It can sound like your own voice, an inner voice or the voice of a guide or spirit. The latter tends to be disjointed and difficult to understand as they have to lower their vibration in order for you to hear them. Clairaudience can also be received as ideas, thoughts or a block of a thought you unravel naturally, often through speech.

Clairsentience – 'Clear feeling.' A person with this skill feels emotions in their body of others or from their supernatural guidance. Healers use this a lot to detect problem areas. It is also a great skill to use to underpin the other skills when interpreting. Example, you see an image of suitcase being packed which could mean many things, but how does it *feel*, in your body? The solar plexus area (upper abdomen) is a common area to sense emotions and feelings. Intuition is intertwined with this skill.

Claircognizance – 'Clear Knowing.' A person with this skill just knows things! They will know information or have a fully formed idea without fully understanding how. They are naturally very wise people. Again, intuition is intertwined with this skill.

There are also two other more rarer forms some people experience.

Clairalience – 'Clear smell.' Receiving guidance through smells. Example, if you have this skill, you might smell a certain fragrance or food which you know is not physically around you. Instead of images or sounds giving you the information or symbolic meaning, you are translating the energy through smell. All types of different smells can be given to you and provide the clues or symbolic meaning you need.

Clairgustance – 'Clear taste.' Receiving the guidance through different tastes and works in the same way as clairalience.

How to Increase Your Abilities.

Levelling up your psychic and intuitive abilities takes a willingness to do so in the first instance and the acceptance it is a constant journey. The following advice to aid your journey may sound simple and basic, but as with most things in life, simple works. The core basics of old are as true today as they have been for hundreds of years.

Incorporate all the below for maximum results, or as many as you wish to or feel comfortable with.

- Meditate.
- Spend time in nature.
- Spend time in your own company and get to know yourself.
- Learn to ground yourself using a method which works for you.
- Stay away from drama, gossip and toxic situations, or at least don't involve yourself in them.
- Learn which of the 'clairs' are your stronger abilities.
- Practice and more practice (more on this below).
- Keep a journal of your practices and developments (more on this below).
- Eat a vegetarian or vegan diet (or mostly).
- Learn from those more established. Take a reputable course.
- Trust yourself and trust the guidance you receive and notice.
- Always ask your guides and supernatural team for more information if you don't understand their messages.

You may wish to get readings from a trusted psychic or medium, which is always a great experience and insightful and I recommend you do it at least once, but there is nothing stopping you doing the same for yourself. This way you can interpret your own guidance for yourself or others as and when you need to. You do after all, have the same ability as the professionals they have just done it longer and are more practised.

Many of these trusted psychic and mediums also offer training. I highly encourage you to do this if it's something you wish to purse with more gusto or you want to go pro and turn into a business.

This is a shorter telegram as it is more of a practical based one and I'm setting you two pieces of continuing work to do.

PRACTICE

Practice, consistency and repetition are key to developing your skills for receiving information, knowing when you are and interpreting it.

Devise separate mini routines for yourself, one for when you meditate or nature walk, and one for when you are tuning in and receiving guidance.

Mediation time shouldn't be used for receiving guidance and messages, this is a sacred time solely to quieten the mind and body. Its impact and benefits compacts over time, that's not to say you might not get a hit of something, but its purpose is for the aforementioned.

Mediation and grounding are also performed prior to tuning in to receiving your guidance to still and quieten the mind, but this is done as an extra to your daily meditation practice. Always meditate and practice your work in a personal space you like and when you know you won't be interrupted.

Only you know how you work best; a lot is trial, and error and your methods will change over time as you become more seasoned at it.

Practice reading other people, either a willing friend or people who are out and about - subtlety of course! For example, when stood in a queue at the supermarket, coffee shop or talking to new people, tune in and try to read their energy. Look past their physical appearance and the words they speak...

How does their energy make you feel?
What does it tell you?
Notice how the energy gives you different feelings and information with different people.

JOURNAL

Keep records and notes in a journal or on a voice recorder. It is useful as often one can forget. I've re read past entries of my own which I had forgotten entirely or had no recollection of writing.

I would advise two journals. One for your psychic work, to note down all the guidance and messages you receive, the information, any symbols, colours and anything you receive back from the supernatural team, and date it. Discount nothing! It might not make sense immediately, but often it will when looking back, like piecing a story together.

A second journal to note down your intuition moments. The signs, gut feelings, insights you get, action you did or didn't take and how it turned out. How you felt, the timings and any patterns.

You can dictate to a voice recorder if this works better for you but keep some sort of notes about your practice and developments. It makes fascinating reading and great fun to look back on.

The More you Practice the Better and Better you Become.

More can always be learnt and developed and if you don't use it, rustiness will set in.

I will write again in a month's time with the final telegram of the year but do keep me posted on your developments and how it works out. This work never ceases to amaze me even though I've personally done it for years.

Let the supernatural team, and yourself, blow your own mind.

Happy tuning in!

The next telegram will arrive 4th December 2021.

The Moon Telegrams

Date: 4th December 2021,
England

Hello to one and all,

The holidays are approaching as is the homestretch in to 2022 and I wanted to round this year off with a telegram topic relevant to the spendy season, and to send you off into 2022 with a positive or interesting view about a loved or loathed topic.

Money and it's symbolism.

Money is a loaded word. I don't need to write about how it touches every aspect of our lives; you already know this, but the symbolism of money and what money <u>actually is</u>, is worth a telegram.

WHAT IS MONEY

Contrary to mass belief, money is not the £10 note in your wallet or the numbers in your bank account. Money is an energy flow, it's a current – currency.

Thousands of years ago coins, notes and bank cards didn't exist. People traded in chickens, cattle, tools and spices for example. Items were bought and sold using these as a way of exchanging services until trading in cattle, and other available sources considered valuable, became impractical and coins were developed. Banks came on the scene as the means to store the coins (the first bank was in Western Turkey around 600 BC). Coins then evolved into paper notes, cheques, bank cards and now digital devices.

How much one has in their wallet or bank account however, is (and always has been) symbolic. Money is a symbol. It's the effect not the cause. It is a representation, the current of a persons' energy and value they hold about themselves.

Your energy is made up of your personal beliefs (past and present), your thoughts and thinking processes, your emotions, expectations, visions, the love and passion for life, the value you hold about yourself and the value you put out into the world. In return, the current of money flows back to you in proportion to your energy and values. It's an energy exchange.

If you find yourself on the lack side of money, or simply want more flowing in, check yourself. Where's your energy at? What do you believe to be true about money? Are you doing what you love? Are you calm and centred or chaotic? Who or what are you surrounded by? Is it positive? ... lack of vision, negativity, doubt, disbelief and hesitancy repel the current of money.

Money is as bigger topic as they come and there are many brilliant teachers on this but hopefully this is enough for you to start questioning where money comes from and why. You must *own* your 'energy' not be owned by *it*... this is ju ju for money. Like success, money is an inside job.

If you still doubt money is a symbolic representation look at bank notes, they are all covered in symbols in some form. Let's look at the American dollar bill before we finish the last Moon Telegram of the year.

AMERICAN DOLLAR BILL

There are numerous power signs and symbols on this note, particularly on its reverse side.

On the front:

There is a picture of the first president of the USA, George Washington. Each note has a different president.

On its reverse:

There is an unfinished pyramid. This pyramid has thirteen steps with a floating smaller pyramid above it. In its centre is the All-Seeing Eye. The triangle and the All-Seeing eye are symbolic of the divine.

There is a picture of the USA's national bird – the bald eagle, both a powerful and exquisite bird. The eagle has a shield in front of it, meaning to rely on one's own virtue.

The eagle's head is surrounded by thirteen stars. The stars are sounded by a cloud or rays of dollar bills, meaning its glory is breaking through the clouds.

The eagle holds a shield in front of it with thirteen bars.

The eagle in its right talons, holds an olive branch representing peace. This branch bears thirteen leaves and thirteen olives. The right side symbolises the dominant side.

In the eagle's left talons, it holds thirteen arrows.

There are three Latin phrases printed on the note:

1. Annuit coeptis, which means 'God has favoured our undertaking.'
2. Novus ordo seclorum, interpreted as 'a new order of the ages.'
3. E pluribus unum, which appears on almost all U.S. coins, and means 'out of many, one.'

The roman numerals translate to 1776, the year America claimed its independence.

It also has the words printed 'In God we Trust' i.e., we trust in an unseen source, whatever that name is for you.

The number thirteen represents the original thirteen states of the USA.

The dollar bill is quite the story, and its symbolism can be broken down further. Have you looked closely at your local currency? I'm sure there a few secrets hidden in plain sight on there for you to gain something from.

It has now come to tend of this telegram on

money and I will sign off the final telegram of 2021.

There will be a break in The Moon Telegrams as I concentrate on my new fiction works coming out, starting this December. Please sign up to my newsletter should this interest you or follow me on my socials, I'd love to see you on one of them or both.

Thank you so much for your readership this year, it's been a joy writing and delivering these each month. I hope they served you and continue to do so.

Don't forget you can purchase The Moon Telegram Books to have them in your back pocket or on your bookshelf and they make perfect stocking fillers!

Wishing you all Happy Holidays, a Merry Christmas and a happy rich healthy filled new year.

P.S

A few famous sayings about money, which combined with the information in this telegram, are sure to make think and look deeper into the mystery...

Scared money doesn't make money.

Money makes a terrible master but an excellent servant.

Are you running your bank account, or is your bank account running you?

Money is simply a tool, so you can live your life as you want to and are supposed to.

Money is a reflection of your self worth.

There is only one source of money (the cosmos, divine) ... but it comes through other people.

Thank you for reading

If you enjoyed The Moon Telegrams or they helped you in anyway, please consider leaving a review it is much appreciated and helps other readers.

Volume one of The Moon Telegrams can be purchased at all major retailers.

Sign up to my newsletter

If you would like to sign up to my newsletter about my fiction works for young and new adults (urban fantasy and contemporary stories) please follow the link below.

https://annaliesemorgan.com/newsletter

In my monthly newsletters you'll be the first to know about all other future titles; continue along with my author and personal life news and chat, behind the scenes information, meet ups and much more!

Connect with Annaliese Morgan

Write:
Annaliese Morgan
49 Greek Street
Soho
London
W1D 4EG

E-Mail:
hello@annaliesemorgan.com

Follow:

annaliese.morgan

annaliesehmorgan

annaliesemorgan.com

Bibliography

Authors own teachings and courses

BBC, The Strange Power of the Evil Eye (https://www.bbc.com/culture/article/20180216-the-strange-power-of-the-evil-eye)

https://www.encyclopedia.com

Hanks, Patrick. (Chief editor). The New Oxford Dictionary of English. (Oxford University Press, 1998)

Morris, Desmond. Bodyguards. (Dorset, UK: Element Books, 1999)

Mountfort, Paul Rhys. Nordic Runes. (Vermont: Destiny Books, 2003)

Norse mythology (https://norse-mythology.org)

Readers Digest (https://www.rd.com/)

Sheildmaidens Sanctum (http://www.shieldmaidenssanctum.com)

Symbol Sage (https://symbolsage.com)

www.ingramcontent.com/pod-product-compliance
Lightning Source LLC
Chambersburg PA
CBHW050045120526
44588CB00037B/2720